AFTERGLOW

Titles also by Michelle Marie Jacquot

Death of a Good Girl

DETERIORATE

AFTERGLOW
MICHELLE MARIE JACQUOT

Copyright © 2022 Michelle Marie Jacquot

www.michellemariejacquot.com

All rights reserved. No part of this book may be reproduced, stored, or transmitted in any form or by any means, electronic, mechanical, photocopying, recording, scanning, or otherwise without written permission from the publisher. It is illegal to copy this book or distribute it by any other means without permission.

Excerpt by Lawrence Ferlinghetti, from POETRY AS INSURGENT ART, copyright ©2007 by Lawrence Ferlinghetti. Reprinted by permission of New Directions Publishing Corp.

Cover photography by Marg

FIRST EDITION

ISBN 978-1-7371427-3-7

CONTENTS

FOREWORD	11
PARTY OF ONE	21
WHEREVER SHE WENT	23
I USED TO HAVE DREAMS	25
MY 2020 PRESIDENTIAL RUN	27
SPLIT ENDS	29
HERE WE ARE NOW, ENTERTAIN US	31
ONGOING UNPRECEDENTED TIMES	33
CUSTOMER SERVICE IN MAY	35
STRANGER	37
WHERE IS MY MIND	39
KNOCK, KNOCK	41
JOKE	43
MEMORY	45
GIRL ALMOST	47
MAYBE HEAVEN GOT BORING	49
I CAN'T STOP READING MY HOROSCOPE	51
EVEN MY TASTEBUDS ARE TURNED OFF	53
TODAY I WANTED TO BREAK A PLATE	55
SOBER GIRL BUYS GROCERIES	57

CONTENTS

MUST LOVE RATS	59
LEMONS	61
HAPPY NEW YEAR, GOD	63
LOOP	65
DEATH POEM	67
DOGS RESEMBLE THEIR OWNERS	69
YOU OWE ME $20	71
AUGUST	73
POMEGRANATES	75
SUPERMOON	77
WISHING SEASON	79
LUCK OF THE ENGLISH	81
YOUTH	83
SUMMER SPENT INSIDE	85
WRITING ON THE WALL	87
GROUNDHOG GIRL	89
SPRING	91
MOTHERHOOD	93
BEAT POETRY ISN'T ALWAYS PRETTY	95
FREEDOM	97
SPEAKING TO THE MANAGER	99
2020'S GREATEST HITS	101

CONTENTS

BUDDHA ON A BICYCLE	103
I CAN ALMOST SMELL THE GRASS	105
GAME NOT OVER	107
DEATH PARTY	109
DEATH X 7	111
JOYEUX ANNIVERSAIRE	113
HAPPY CHRISTMAS	115
VOTE JOHN LENNON AS GOD'S REPLACEMENT	117
EPIPHANY	119
BIBLICAL	121
RELIGION	123
GRAB JOY WHERE YOU CAN GET IT	125
DIVING WITH HAFEZ	127
WOMEN AREN'T FUNNY	129
TWO THINGS CAN BE TRUE	131
GÖKOTTA	133
EARTHQUAKE WEATHER	135
DOG YEARS	137
LIFETIMES	139
A PLACE I'D LIKE TO GO	141
IMAGINE	143
ABOUT THE AUTHOR	147

"For a long time it had seemed to me that life was about to begin—real life. But there was always some obstacle in the way, something to be got through first, some unfinished business, time still to be served, a debt to be paid. Then life would begin. At last it dawned on me that these obstacles were my life."

—ALFRED D'SOUZA

FOREWORD

I'm writing this in late May of 2022. I'm in Joshua Tree, sitting on a concrete floor in a little white room out in the middle of the desert, surrounded by almost nothing. It feels like an ocean. I came here to finish this book. Mercury is in retrograde, if that means anything to you. I'm not sure if it does to me. There's dirt and bugs for miles, and not much else. It's perfect—as perfect as it's ever going to be. I started writing these poems in early 2020, when everything started going to shit. I then realized (not as quickly as I would have liked, but eventually) that everything is always, somehow, going to shit. Everything is, at the same time, always coming together. There's never a moment in life when it just stands completely still, even if that's the way it feels.

My first instinct was to never publish this book, it seemed too big a burden to give to people who had already lived it, to then ask them to read about it. My next instinct was to wait until the pandemic was over. And then it kept going. And going. And going—until it looked like it would never end. I wanted to call it "Afterlife" for a while, because I naively thought I would be able to separate my life into two parts. One that had already happened, and now that everything was paused, another for the one that would come next. As if life were something that could be stopped or started at any designated time. Some different existence out beyond the months spent staring at a wall, one that had late nights and long days and new experiences, grand beginnings—that would suddenly commence the second this nonexistent "someday" bubble burst, when everything was normal and good again. Nothing is ever "normal and good," you see?

It became clear there would be no "back to life," we were here and we had been living it the entire time. The only thing we're really given is the opportunity to make the most of what time there is left on this giant, spinning rock. It's ridiculous—the whole thing. Ridiculous and beautiful, so finite yet infinite, it's almost hilarious. If I've learned anything from observing the sky over the last few years, it's that the sun never waits on better conditions to rise. It shows up every day, no matter what else is going on around it. I've learned to laugh at everything, that it might be the only real thing that matters. I know that each time the sun goes down, an afterglow exists—should you choose to see it. And if you never did before, make a different choice. There's another sunset happening tonight, and if it already has by the time you're reading this, wake up early.

I'm pulled over on the side of the road now as I write this. It's golden hour. There's a good chance I miss the sunset I drove all the way here for. I'm on my way back into town to get dinner, no matter how hard I tried to convince myself I would be fine if I didn't. I got to this deserted house much later than I thought I would and didn't realize how far it was from civilization. I had wanted so badly to get here, unpack, settle in and write this introduction when everything was calm, but that's not happening. I wasn't given that option today, not really. But I know what to say right now, on the shoulder of this dirt road, starving as I lose the sun, because it works that way. Jesus or God or Madonna take the wheel, or whatever. I was almost born in the back of a car for the same reason.

Life is a mess. It doesn't go on once you get home at a reasonable hour and neatly fold your clothes. It happens in the middle of something important, when you're running late to church or at a party or leaving the place you should have stayed just five minutes longer, unknown to you. There are road bumps and hazards and closures, some that last two years or more, and you can't control any of it. The only thing you can do is laugh or write or just keep going, all of which I tried my best at. I hope any of these sometimes silly, sometimes sad, sometimes hope-filled poems put some life back into what felt like a very strange time for all of us. This book may well be just an odd time capsule. But I wanted to give these poems space to exist, because they happened and they're true and I want to include every piece of our existence in the story.

The road back to where I'm staying is lined with streets that have the word "sun" in them. Sunbeam, Sunkist, Sunfair, Sun Gold, Sunever—which I read as "never" on my way in and "ever" on the way out. Funny how perspectives change like that. There are more, if you can believe it: Sun Mesa, Sunflower, Sunny Vista, Avenida Del Sol, Sundra—which I can only assume is some sort of sun tundra, which I can only assume I'm completely wrong about. The last street is called Shifting Sands, and they are, I can feel it.

I didn't miss the sunset. But if I had, it wouldn't have mattered. It would still be light out. And often, that's the best part, the part that happens after. It's where the most magnificent colors come from. If I hadn't made it back in time for whatever I had made up in my mind was the main event, there would have been an afterglow. And if that was all I was promised from that point moving forward, I was going to take it, and savour it, however long it lasted.

The definition of afterglow is "a glow remaining where a light has disappeared." I believe that glow is always present, should you keep your eyes open and stay on the lookout for it. If I may leave you with one task, it's this: I ask that you spend your life not chasing one that's already happened, not looking ahead to one not promised, but taking in every ounce of this one, the one you have right here, right now in your palm, and spend the whole thing laughing. I hope you enjoy this book even though, honestly, most of the poems have nothing to do with this. We'll get there in the end. I hope you think that's funny in itself, because I do. Because I felt like I needed to write this regardless, for both of us. Because I love this book, I believe everything that happened matters, I believe in making jokes, and at the time of finishing this foreword—I'm sitting in the light of the sun that set well over an hour ago, and God, no matter how I got here, I wouldn't want to be anywhere else.

P.S. If you don't like the word "God," stay away from this book. I don't know if I like it either, but I use the hell out of it.

P.P.S. I just looked up what "Sundra" means, turns out it's just a name. I didn't really even remember what the tundra was, which I'm blaming on growing up in Southern California. After some fifth-grade geography style research, I'm reminded it's the world's harshest biome, a frozen region in the Arctic. It's the coldest place in the world. It's also considered a desert, funny enough. The winters are hard, there's a permanent layer of ice that stays frozen no matter what. The sun rarely comes out, but when it does, it stays for almost twenty-four hours. They call it the "land of the midnight sun." Summers are brief, lasting about two months, and when they arrive, wildflowers come in bursts. They bloom quickly and miraculously, in a way that would make you think they either have no idea they're going to die so soon, or that they do know and it's the only thing they're living by (or maybe they're just unafraid, know they'll be back in another life). In conditions that seem inhospitable, inconceivable for anything to be born into, let alone thrive, they do. Even in the coldest place on Earth, there are invincible summers, growth seasons, life still to be found.

"The North Pole is not where it used to be."

—LAWRENCE FERLINGHETTI

(1919–2021)

PARTY OF ONE

I had my birthday party
indoors this year
So did everyone else
in the entire world, I hear

Maybe I'm not as depressingly special as I thought

Maybe we've all been secretly eating cake
alone in the dark all along

WHEREVER SHE WENT

You know when people go to sleep
and never wake up again?

That's how I feel about whoever I was
at the beginning of this year

I USED TO HAVE DREAMS

I had a dream
once

I don't anymore

How did Martin Luther King
survive all he did when I can't even
get out of bed to make a bowl of cereal
if I got less than six hours of sleep?

MY 2020 PRESIDENTIAL RUN

I found out this morning
I've grown crow's feet on my face
I'm another year older and it shows
and all I did was blink
and cry and scream and read the news

You could have sworn I'd gone through a presidency
or a very bad divorce

SPLIT ENDS

I bought scissors in April
to celebrate the split
it worked for a while
but now I'm frozen in this flat
with both my personalities
one who hates short hair and thinks she's British
says words like "flat" when she knows she says
"apartment" out loud, wishes her roots would grow in
quicker, the other wishes she didn't care

I can feel the summer coming, my hair's finally
unblue and long enough for someone else to pull
That's a custody battle I'd love to lose

I never even got divorced, I'm not sure why I talk like that
or why I act like I've spent my entire life sitting in court

I only cut off all my hair and dyed it blue, something
a lawyer or a husband surely would have advised me
to never ever ever ever ever ever do

HERE WE ARE NOW, ENTERTAIN US

Who would have thought
Politics
Would be the one thing going back to normal

Even old men blowing up the world is getting boring

ONGOING UNPRECEDENTED TIMES

Genuine question;

In history, has there ever been
a precedented one?

Nothing ever happens
until it does

Say "unprecedented"
one more time, I dare you
I'll crash my car
and unprecedent
your driver's side
door into a wall

At least there's a new president
who knows the alphabet, I hope
Who can count backwards from 5
when the bombs finally explode

That wouldn't be unprecedented, either.

CUSTOMER SERVICE IN MAY

God, what I would give
to take back all the jobs I hate
to see another human in the flesh
even if I wanted to punch them in the face

STRANGER

A stranger said he "liked my sweater"
I forgot what it felt like to be complimented
So for a second, I enjoyed it, until I remembered
No, I didn't. Or at least whoever
I was at the beginning
wouldn't

But maybe, strong maybe
That's not who I want to be now
Maybe I'm a stranger to us both
Maybe I like me this way better

I have no clues, one way or the other
or if I even still like my own sweater
It doesn't fit now, that's for sure
If there's one thing I do know
Thanks, Oprah

I wonder how long this kind of person stands in front of the mirror, if she has the same amount of road rage, gets out of her car to yell at strangers on the freeway, what time she tells herself she'll wake up in the morning, if she's still allergic to tree nuts, common decency and sports

WHERE IS MY MIND

I don't know what a heart attack feels like
but I just watched a lizard climb inside my house
and immediately stated writing a poem about it
instead of trying to get it back out

KNOCK, KNOCK

Can someone let me in on the plan?
I'm getting pretty goddamn tired
of recycling these memories
since they're the only ones I have

JOKE

All my pens are running out of ink,
is this some kind of stupid metaphor?

MEMORY

Does anybody remember laughter?

No, stop asking

GIRL ALMOST

Does—

But doesn't

Doesn't what?

Exactly

It'll all be gone tomorrow
But no one thought to warn us
There'll be nothing left to make fun of
Or have a take on, even if you wanted

Even the stand-up comedians
Got the same feeling I did
That nothing's funny anymore
And might not ever be again

MAYBE HEAVEN GOT BORING

I saw an ant today on my balcony ledge
and I didn't want to kill him, yet
So I blew him off and he flew
from the second floor and I think
it gave him the biggest thrill of his sad little life

He looked light as a feather, I don't think
he would have died, or else I never would have
done it, or maybe would have, for the story

From now on, he'll be known as the First Ant
in History to fly. He'll tell all his ant friends about his
airbrush with death, how he broke a new ant record
and survived to see it in print

You're welcome, Ant.

Now I know how God feels
I nearly killed him, probably ruined his day
Broke his leg at the very least, then said
"you're welcome" and really thought
I did a good thing

Gave myself a pat on the back
for almost murdering something, purely
for fun, then at the last second, taking it back

I'm not really sure how I feel about anyone
having the whole world in their hands

I CAN'T STOP READING MY HOROSCOPE

My neighbor addresses everyone in apartment numbers, so
I'm eleven, in numerology that means I've ascended from
hell and into heaven, like Aldous Huxley either said was
destiny or bullshit, I still don't understand which one

I'm living in both, not sure if either exist, doing everything
backwards, trying my best to get to Kent from Los Angeles
for whatever reason, which proved my worst idea yet

Everyone here is on hard drugs, I am so insanely sober
I feel nuts. Like I am the only one not seeing clearly because
of it, this permanent haze become reality and my horoscope
is always wrong but I'm still reading it as gospel

EVEN MY TASTEBUDS ARE TURNED OFF

I sit inside
with nothing else
to do but reminisce
I'd go outside if they let me
but they won't, or so I tell myself
I just keep sitting in the same spot, taste testing
my own tears, having fits of laughter turned to grief over
absolutely nothing until it all melts together
and I can't tell the difference anymore
between
what's funny
what's sad and
what's just plain salt

TODAY I WANTED TO BREAK A PLATE

Today I wanted to break a plate
to have some proof
I had control over things
To make a cult of broken shapes
Piece them back together
Act like they were meant that way
Like it would all work out, somehow
better than before. Google "shattered glass"
and "good omens" like it was my new 9 to 5 job
Put chaos in its place, finally find its rightful drawer
Tell myself no matter what I lost, something new
was on the way. I'd believe in something else
if it was the last thing I ever did. I'd break
every plate in my house, if I had to
It's not a metaphor
I can, and I did

SOBER GIRL BUYS GROCERIES

There's acid sparkling down my throat
and in the tips of every finger
and ends of all my toes
doing whatever the opposite
of tiptoeing does
I'm licking it all off politely
until it's so clean that it's dirty
and so repulsive even the men with
foot fetishes wouldn't touch it
Obsessions built in afternoon reminders
of who I thought I used to be but clearly never got rid of
entirely, because it's 3PM and I've ended up sitting on
my kitchen counter again, staring out the window
glorifying some bread and a toaster
licking jam until there's nothing less than nothing left and
I've decided
for today, at least
I'm done wasting my life
eating myself half to death
inhaling sugar like it's acid
and I am on a midnight binge

All my addictions are legal, in fact
they're sold right in grocery stores
Which should make it sound better
but it just makes it so much worse

MUST LOVE RATS

There's nothing tangible to see here
of anything that took a breath
The only thing I have to prove the love
that almost happened is

These moldy tangerine skins
I haven't taken out the trash
for weeks because of it

He tastes like rotting oranges now
And you know I've always been a sucker
for a good man going bad

LEMONS

He was the first person to ask if I'd heard about it,
replacing the C with a Q
Right before it all went down, around the same time
he went to Quintana Roo
On holiday, the name of my favorite author's
only daughter

How dare he know who I was so deeply
without ever knowing at all

Drinking coronas with lime on a beach, making light
of such life-altering things

How dare he make me squeeze my White Album out before
I was ready, hold onto it for so long that all its pages
yellowed

HAPPY NEW YEAR, GOD

This was the year
I thought I lost the love of my life
and that love came with a price
of the life of the dreams I used to have
and I don't know if I'll ever get to see them again
and each day it all slips further and further and quicker
and faster and I don't think my arms will ever
be strong enough to reach them again
and it kills me
and I know full well people are dying by the minute
by the day and I'm able, but what's the difference
when I feel like a dead girl walking anyway?
Haunt my own home's halls in a body I no longer control
where I have nothing left inside or out to do or say or think
I'm just a gut and a skull sleeping in a canyon that I hate
that I used to love when I was younger, but I'm older
and I'm here and I almost throw up every day
It rained when I moved in, I ignored it
and every single bad sign that followed
and that very long day turned into a very long year
that I know once I'm gone I'll only think about fast and slow
it all was and how all I lived about was what I ate and how I
lost and the weight I didn't and what I gained
which wasn't anything important
or worth noting
and I didn't write it down if it was
at least I attempted to attempt to say
something
here

I think
but it's not the thought that counts
and that's the only thing I learned this year

(which was my biggest fear of all
and then that fear came to life
and it really was as bad as I had always thought
maybe even worse
and then it died, and God is cruel
So he kept me alive to watch it all burn
and go to hell
Thanks a lot, God
I bet you got made fun of a lot in school)

LOOP

Today: I love you, my life will be meaningless
without you
Tomorrow: I hate you, your life will be meaningless
without me

1) Take your pick
2) Repeat until you can't
and you always can,
that son of a bitch

DEATH POEM

I was meeting him while I was putting out my
death book (because of course I was)

He sat on my shelf for months on end, saying he wanted
to read every word, never did, never would, never
got around to it (didn't have the capacity or
shelf life, he knew that but never said it
kept it to himself for good measure)

Only touched, grazed the spine for a few brief, glorious
seconds, placed it back as if he never said a word, was
never even mentioned (he'd never admit that)

Thumbing through bodies like books upstairs at City Lights
but the mind thumbing was worse, if you can call it that (you
shouldn't, sounds stupid)

Like giving your opinion on a movie you know you've never
watched, never would, even if someone bought you the box
set for Christmas (he wouldn't want to, wasn't religious)

He never knew me much, at the heart of it
I was a dead girl then, and dead girls don't have spare organs
for loaning out like libraries, you know

I've changed my mind and died many
times over since then, I don't know him
anymore, don't know if I ever did

He's been busy walking dogs and taking the same photo over and over again, with his always-more-famous-than-him girlfriend—this time, blonde

He never loved me, only wanted me to meet his parents

Started rotting out the second my roots started growing in, wanted nothing to do with it (thank God)

If only I had known back then that Death was the luckiest card in the deck

DOGS RESEMBLE THEIR OWNERS

You have the life of your own dreams now
And it looks very different to the one I had
The one in my vision never had any dogs
But you and her have two
Both ugly, if I'm honest
You know what they say

YOU OWE ME $20

If you never loved me,
the Tooth Fairy is real

AUGUST

You can't grow new leaves while the old ones
are still falling, despite appearances
it takes time, dying

POMEGRANATES

I am sick to death of feeling such deep, rotting
sadness. I've had enough pits in my stomach in one lifetime
to feed the whole world with pomegranates

SUPERMOON

If the worst comes to the worst, at least tonight's a blue
moon, I used to hate that color, always tying it to you

They say it's super this time, that's nice of them, I guess
We may be underwater, but at least we know how to swim

Taurus season came and went, I stopped driving to the
beaches, got sick of everything I loved slipping through my
hands, breaking my own good memories to glass pieces

If nothing else were to come from this bull year by the ocean,
at least I noticed it was you I never needed, not my boy blue

Thank God for changing tides, time passing, and lifelong
devotion—big bodies of water that bring us back to when the
world felt small and favorite colors were important decisions

WISHING SEASON

By the time my hair grows down my back
By the time I hate it, then cut it all off

By the time I lose the last ten pounds
Then they'll see they really missed out

By the time the blonde in my fringe is gone
By the time you love me, I won't be me at all

I've heard about living, and it sounds real fun
Maybe one day I'll do it when my waiting is done

Hope I get to a beach before they all wash up
By the time I reread this, hope it's not all gone

Hope I didn't give myself another God
awful haircut, on second thought

Hope I did, life's too short

LUCK OF THE ENGLISH

While the whole world was sleeping
for three-hundred sixty-five days on end
The grass turned green and every clover
turned over and grew four leaves

Even with the whole history repeating
thing, no one learned the lesson, no one
kissed under the mistletoe or made a single
wish. There was luck by the handful, like this
town had never seen, and it was true, no one did

What a shame, the whole world showing off
for no reason, all that good luck gone to waste
All the four-leaf clovers that got dressed up
and ended up having no one to impress

YOUTH

Combing through a memory
Of the blonde curls I once had
If my eyes close long enough
I can still hold it in my hand

Running circles through the grass
With a net that was a wand
Chasing butterflies and dragons
That were only little moths

I never knew they weren't big enough
And might not ever grow to be
Catching gold dust in the backyard
Praying it might stick on me

That was all I ever wanted
So then I would set them free
Maybe I could live forever
How violet I would be

In my garden I was safe
From all life's violent little truths
Where I would never hurt a fly
A fly would never hurt me, too

You could never tell me otherwise
Living under that pink moon
Where the moths were always butterflies
The sky would never not be blue

SUMMER SPENT INSIDE

One summer has come and gone
Without the melting of my skin
From laying underneath the sun
For hours on deadly end

Fry my insides out
To turn someone else on
Burning one shade darker
Risking cancer for fun

One whole year has passed
I've done none of the above
Maybe I'll spend more time
With the moon, fuck the sun

Take no more skin off my back
At the expense of a crush
Think I'll stay myself again
Each time next summer comes

WRITING ON THE WALL

A strange phenomenon it is
To spend a whole year in a place
You never even got to live
But have to move out all the same

I'm only just arriving
It's already time to leave
I'm packing up a living room
Where I did no such thing

Taking photos off the shelves
From a life I didn't get to keep
Sitting on the hollow floor
Filling boxes only just emptied

I've seen nothing but these halls
For weeks and months on end
They didn't speak like I had hoped
I wish they had at least pretended

How badly do I wish
I left some writing on these walls
or blood or paint or proof of living
or of anything at all

GROUNDHOG GIRL

I'm looking forward
to cherry picking stories
of the good parts of this place
Selecting memories and pretending
the seasons were welcome, or ever changed
As far as I was aware, spring never actually came
Summer never happened, winter never ended, no fruit
went ripe, I didn't even realize my lease was up until the
animal in the ground popped its head out and told me it was

I got to live in my dream house for a while, and every month
was October. There was possibility and perfect weather every
day, birds never woke me up, and I loved all my neighbors

I'll be cherry picking stories like a real Groundhog Girl does
Every day was my luckiest, every day in those hills had sun
At the edge of my street, which was the edge of the world
As far as I was ever concerned back when I was a real good

SPRING

If I could list all the things I did here
in a year, the list would be too long, but
I'll tell you what I learned from nature

Outside my door, a mother bird built a nest
that she kicked her own eggs out of after
an entire spring of protecting them

I wasn't shocked, I'm not writing songs
like I used to, I'm not writing songs at all
I know how it feels to not want the one
thing you're supposed to love

I played a million chords this year, then
threw them up into the sky. They never
came back down, and it's a mystery
how time flies

I don't even know where they went, maybe
never to be heard again. I'm not writing
music like I used to, why would I
want to after this?

MOTHERHOOD

How it feels to write a book
is not like having a baby
It's much worse, you hate the thing

Maybe it is like having a baby.

BEAT POETRY ISN'T ALWAYS PRETTY

I tried to make these poems nicer
have happier endings, after the fact
But the fact is, it only made them
worse. This is the truth, not as it is
but as it was, and the truth of each
moment is all that should ever exist

FIRST WORD, BEST WORD
I LOVE YOU, ALLEN GINSBERG

All my idols are dying
Normal people are dying
Lawrence Ferlinghetti lived to be 101
He always did have perfect timing

FREEDOM

I'm looking forward to being
just
being
Free at last, free for the chance
to fall in love
to fall in hate
to fuck the world
Fall in lukewarm water, go home
take a shower, shake it all off
and forget the next day
Free to start again and dance
to songs that don't mean
a goddamn thing

I'll be daydreaming about daydreaming about the day when
I'll get to smile at strangers on the street without covering
my face, even though I liked that part secretly

I won't be using my new wings to spread any kind of
kindness, it's just the freedom that I'm after
and I'll pay whatever the cost

SPEAKING TO THE MANAGER

Some years shouldn't count
Some years go too far
Find out too much about you
Might not keep their mouths shut

Some years are kids on bikes
Passing by before you know it
Youth isn't wasted on the young
We tried to spend it, we just couldn't

The year my body didn't add any bodies
to its count, just one more lap around the sun
praying my last gasps of collagen and freedom
wouldn't be gone by the time it came back around

Some years shouldn't count
toward the hundred-year total
If this one was stolen like it was
shouldn't we get some sort of discount?

Some twenties back, at least
Some store credit for the trouble
Please, let me speak to the manager
Let me tell him I'm a local

2020'S GREATEST HITS

It hurts more to pretend
than it does to admit
Looking back will only
ever break your neck

BUDDHA ON A BICYCLE

Why are you under the impression
that this thing you wake up and take part in
every morning is not your life?

Is someone else's, is just some motions
that don't count, and won't until the timing is right
which will be, surprise—NEVER

You are not leasing a house, you are living a life.

Why are you so sure that the one you move into
after this will finally be the one you wanted?

When will what goes through your eyes and out your nose
finally sink into your skin?

When will you finally hear that TODAY doesn't mean
TOMORROW—today has almost already happened
and yesterday was never tomorrow's problem

ACT NOW, TIME IS RUNNING FAST
                                      BUT IT HAS NOT
                              RUN OUT

I CAN ALMOST SMELL THE GRASS

I was waiting for anything to happen
Someone to tell me what came next
It felt so pointless then, praying
But how many lives we get

The unimaginable paths
We have not walked on yet
No one can say what goes on there
I wouldn't want to hear it if they did

We'll meet those days as they unfold
But for now, it's time to rest
And be sure to get a good night's sleep
For the living times ahead

GAME NOT OVER

They say it ain't over til the fat lady sings
Good thing I stopped making music,
started doing stand-up comedy

DEATH PARTY

You have approximately ten thousand
eight hundred and four breaths left
Make sure you use them all
exhaustively, to death

There may be an after party, but we
aren't sure if we're invited yet
So never plan your moves
according to that

DEATH X 7

Death death death death death death death

Are you ready?

Okay, no more of that (until we get to heaven, maybe)

JOYEUX ANNIVERSAIRE

All I want for Christmas Eve is to feel something again
An angel to sing "Happy Birthday" from the rooftop
in French, and mean it

Like my last name is the only language left they believe in

Want to act like they almost named me Noël for good reason

HAPPY CHRISTMAS

War is over, if you want it
and Dear God, I want it bad

VOTE JOHN LENNON AS GOD'S REPLACEMENT

War is over, if you want it
and Dear God, I want it bad
Dear God, it's me, Margaret
Are you listening? Are you dead?
Did the phone lines lose connection?
WAR'S NOT OVER, GET BACK OUT OF BED
YOU ASKED AND I POLITELY SAID I WANTED IT
REAL BAD. IT'S CHRISTMAS, YOU SHOULD KNOW
BETTER, WE'VE ALL BEEN GOOD ALL YEAR LONG

IS GOD GONE? IS HE OUT OF OFFICE? HAS HE
BEEN HANGING OUT WITH BORIS JOHNSON?

EPIPHANY

You know what? I'm just thinking out loud—I've never
seen Santa Claus and God in the same room, not once

BIBLICAL

Jesus Christ, am I biblical
for someone who doesn't
even believe in God

RELIGION

I BELIEVE IN CHANGE, EVEN IF CHANGE
DOESN'T BELIEVE I EXIST
EVEN IF I'M JUST A GHOST STORY FOR IT
TO LAUGH AT WITH ITS FRIENDS

EVEN IF IT THINKS I'VE DIED ALREADY, THE THING
IT DOESN'T KNOW ABOUT ME IS
I'M A GEMINI RISING, I WILL ALWAYS FIND A WAY
TO RESURRECT

THEY'VE SAID THE EARTH HAS BEEN ENDING
A THOUSAND TIMES BEFORE
I KNOW IT WILL ONE DAY, BUT ONE DAY
WON'T BE THIS MORNING

WHY WOULD I LET THE APOCALYPSE
THAT'S COMING LONG AFTER I'M GONE
SPOIL MY COFFEE? YOU KNOW I DIDN'T GO
TO ALICE'S RESTAURANT FOR NOTHING

IT IS SO QUIET IT'S RIDICULOUS, I CAN'T STOP
LAUGHING TO MYSELF
HAVE YOU EVER PRAYED OUT LOUD TO NO ONE
JUST TO HEAR THE SOUND?

THE DAY HAS BARELY STARTED, I'M BASKING
IN THIS DESERT HEAT
LISTENING TO JUNE THIS MORNING, I HAVE ALL
THE FAITH I'LL EVER NEED

I DON'T CARE HOW MANY LIVES IT TAKES
I'M GOING TO GET WHAT I CAME DOWN FOR
TRY TO REMEMBER THAT I SPENT THE FIRST
FIFTEEN YEARS OF THIS ONE AS A DANCER

THIS LIFE IS TOO WILD TO BE PRECIOUS WITH,
AND JUST IN CASE THERE'S NOT ONE AFTER—
WHEN MARY OLIVER ASKS WHAT I'M GOING
TO DO WITH IT, I WANT TO HAVE AN ANSWER

I DON'T KNOW HOW MANY DAYS I HAVE LEFT
I'M GOING TO MAKE THEM ALL COUNT
NOT WASTE THEM DANCING AROUND
RETROGRADES, ASTROLOGY CAN FUCK ITSELF

MAYBE THE WORLD HAS GIVEN UP ON ME, AND
IF IT HAS—SO BE IT. I STILL WAKE UP BEFORE
THE SUN, IF YOU CAN'T JOIN IT, BEAT IT

I BELIEVE IN CHANGE, EVEN IF IT DOESN'T
MATTER. EVEN IF IT COUNTS ME OUT, TELLS ME
I'M NOT EVEN IN THE RUNNING, I WILL ONLY
RUN FASTER

I BELIEVE CHANGE IS COMING
I BELIEVE WITH MY WHOLE BODY
I SAW THE MOON TODAY IN BROAD DAYLIGHT
AND JESUS CHRIST, THE GLOW WAS
UNBELIEVABLE

GRAB JOY WHERE YOU CAN GET IT

I can't wait to own my own house—just so I can keep the
        Christmas lights up all year round. Everyone will say
                I went insane, I'll wonder why they didn't
                      Am I the only one who knows
                how fun it is to sing along with
        Elvis in your kitchen?
                        I'll have my White Christmas
              in the middle of summer, in this house
        you'll never need an excuse to celebrate with
    Nat King Cole, get a yacht with Eartha Kitt or swing
to Fats Domino, and board games are always encouraged

DIVING WITH HAFEZ

The part they never tell you is how much patience
comes before the jump, I just remembered I was in

chess club when I was eleven and had a pet turtle
growing up. Truth is, I'm a fantastic liar, but I swear

both these things are true. I haven't changed anything
yet this morning—why would I want to, when I could

go swimming instead? I still have the whole day
ahead of me, a thousand serious moves left

WOMEN AREN'T FUNNY

I am obsessed with mornings, apparently
But I wish these birds would just shut up
They are so beautiful and loud about it, it's
annoying, makes me feel bad about myself

Oh—I understand these idiots now. If only
they understood themselves. They can take
their boring dick jokes, and much like
astrology, fuck themselves

TWO THINGS CAN BE TRUE

I'm taller now
I didn't measure
It was just something I knew

GÖKOTTA

There is much to smile about
Though there is much yet to be done
For there is always soap in the kitchen
And trees out in the yard

No one will fall ill
If you go to the shops for lunch
Take an extra hour
To taste the cinnamon on your tongue

There's a reason we retire
A season to feel young
For a moment we can pretend
There are no wars left to be won

Let yourself sit quiet
Hear the wind inside your lungs
Pay attention to the birds
While you still understand their songs

Today our eyes have opened
And that shall be enough
For there will always be soap in the kitchen
And trees out in the yard

EARTHQUAKE WEATHER

Eleven straight days of sun
after twelve hard weeks of snow
It's all finally starting to look up,
what do you know!

Forward and on, like a bunch of
HOT PINK HAPPY BIRTHDAY BALLOONS
It should all be coming up
ROSES
sometime
pretty
soon

I like my predictions coming from men with pointer sticks,
wearing tuxes like magicians, standing in front of huge
holographic maps—now look at the stars again and
tell me which religion seems more ridiculous

I know it won't last long, but tonight, let's enjoy it.

Let's pretend whatever he says goes, that weather never
changes. Kiss me hard like the world knows something we
don't about the rain, like we're almost out of chances

DOG YEARS

After twenty-six years, I've met myself again here
My life laid out on the floor, this empty house, these woods
where it's just me and me and me and all my poetry bags

As if I've lived a thousand years, as if I packed to move
to France—and still could, where growing old and changing
course has always been a gift, not a curse

Every early morning and dark circle has been worth it
I would thank them if I could, but there are just too many
A thousand more poem wrinkles to go, God willing

LIFETIMES

I cannot wait
to have all white hair
Can you imagine the wisdom
in all those years?

How many lives lived
in just one woman
I cannot wait to
be that clear

A PLACE I'D LIKE TO GO

I just found out "Lennon" rhymes with "Heaven"
I bet they say "thank Yoko" there

IMAGINE

I dare you to imagine
A place where everything goes right
One where the voices in your head
Only tell stories that you like

One where every new hello
Didn't promise endings or goodbye
Your poor heart became so rich
You learned to dance instead of cry

What if all the hopes you had here
Were not just dreams of another life?
What if the worst had already come to pass
And everything, from here on out, went terribly

                                                                right?

ABOUT THE AUTHOR

Michelle Marie Jacquot is a writer from Los Angeles, California. Her debut poetry collection *Death of a Good Girl* was published in 2019, followed by *DETERIORATE* in 2021. She's also a stand-up comedian, actress, songwriter, and singer—because in case you forgot, she's a Gemini rising Capricorn. She was born on Christmas Eve in a Seventh-day Adventist Church hospital that doesn't serve coffee, because of course she was. She unironically loves 90's country music, for good measure.

◎ *@michellemariejacquot*
🐦 *@michellejacquot*
www.michellemariejacquot.com

www.ingramcontent.com/pod-product-compliance
Lightning Source LLC
Chambersburg PA
CBHW030303100526
44590CB00012B/497